EIGHTH NOTE PUBLICATIONS

Chorus No. 1
from Christmas Oratorio

Johann Sebastian Bach
Arranged by David Marlatt

One of the most famous compositions of Johann Sebastian Bach (1685-1750) is his *Christmas Oratorio* BWV 248. This large-scale work was composed for the Christmas season of 1734-35 and Bach used material from three recently composed cantatas (BWV 213, 214 and 215). The original work was composed for an ensemble consisting of flutes, oboes, oboes d'amore, bassoons, horns, trumpets, timpani, strings, continuo and choir.

ISBN: 9781771578493
CATALOG NUMBER: TE221268

COST: $20.00
DURATION: 7:55

DIFFICULTY RATING: Difficult
3 Trumpets and Keyboard

www.enpmusic.com

CHORUS No. 1

from CHRISTMAS ORATORIO
Jauchzet, frohlocket, auf, preiset die Tage

J.S. Bach
(1685-1750)
Arranged by David Marlatt

CHORUS No. 1 *from* CHRISTMAS ORATORIO pg. 2

CHORUS No. 1 *from* CHRISTMAS ORATORIO pg. 3

CHORUS No. 1 *from* CHRISTMAS ORATORIO pg. 4

CHORUS No. 1 *from* CHRISTMAS ORATORIO pg. 5

CHORUS No. 1
from CHRISTMAS ORATORIO
Jauchzet, frohlocket, auf, preiset die Tage

J.S. Bach
(1685-1750)
Arranged by David Marlatt

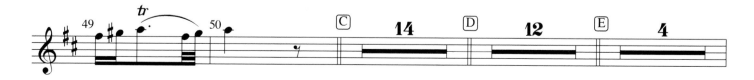

CHORUS No. 1 *from* CHRISTMAS ORATORIO pg. 2

CHORUS No. 1

C Trumpet 2
Piccolo part provided

from CHRISTMAS ORATORIO
Jauchzet, frohlocket, auf, preiset die Tage

J.S. Bach
(1685-1750)
Arranged by David Marlatt

CHORUS No. 1 *from* CHRISTMAS ORATORIO pg. 2

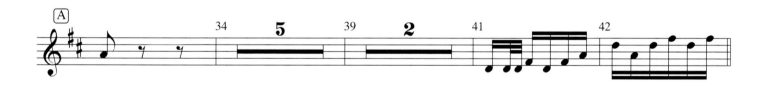

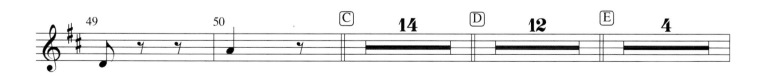

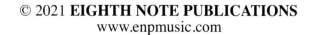

CHORUS No. 1

A Piccolo Trumpet 1

from CHRISTMAS ORATORIO
Jauchzet, frohlocket, auf, preiset die Tage

J.S. Bach
(1685-1750)
Arranged by David Marlatt

CHORUS No. 1

A Piccolo Trumpet 2

from CHRISTMAS ORATORIO
Jauchzet, frohlocket, auf, preiset die Tage

J.S. Bach
(1685-1750)
Arranged by David Marlatt

CHORUS No. 1

A Piccolo Trumpet 3

from CHRISTMAS ORATORIO
Jauchzet, frohlocket, auf, preiset die Tage

J.S. Bach
(1685-1750)
Arranged by David Marlatt

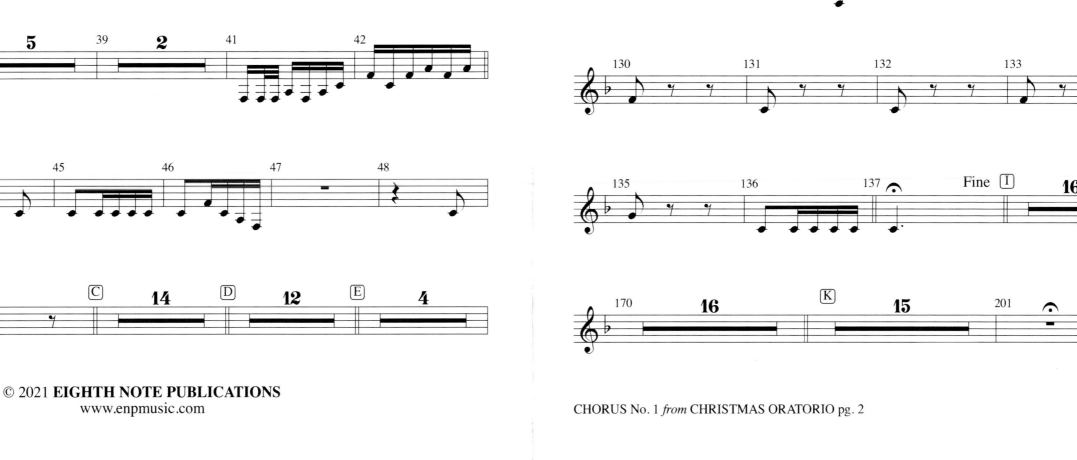

CHORUS No. 1

Timpani

from CHRISTMAS ORATORIO
Jauchzet, frohlocket, auf, preiset die Tage

J.S. Bach
(1685-1750)
Arranged by David Marlatt

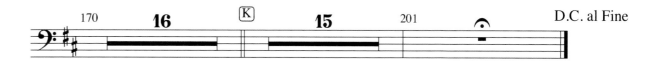

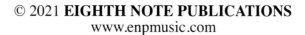

CHORUS No. 1 *from* CHRISTMAS ORATORIO pg. 7

CHORUS No. 1 *from* CHRISTMAS ORATORIO pg. 8

CHORUS No. 1 *from* CHRISTMAS ORATORIO pg. 9

CHORUS No. 1 *from* CHRISTMAS ORATORIO pg. 10